D1535779

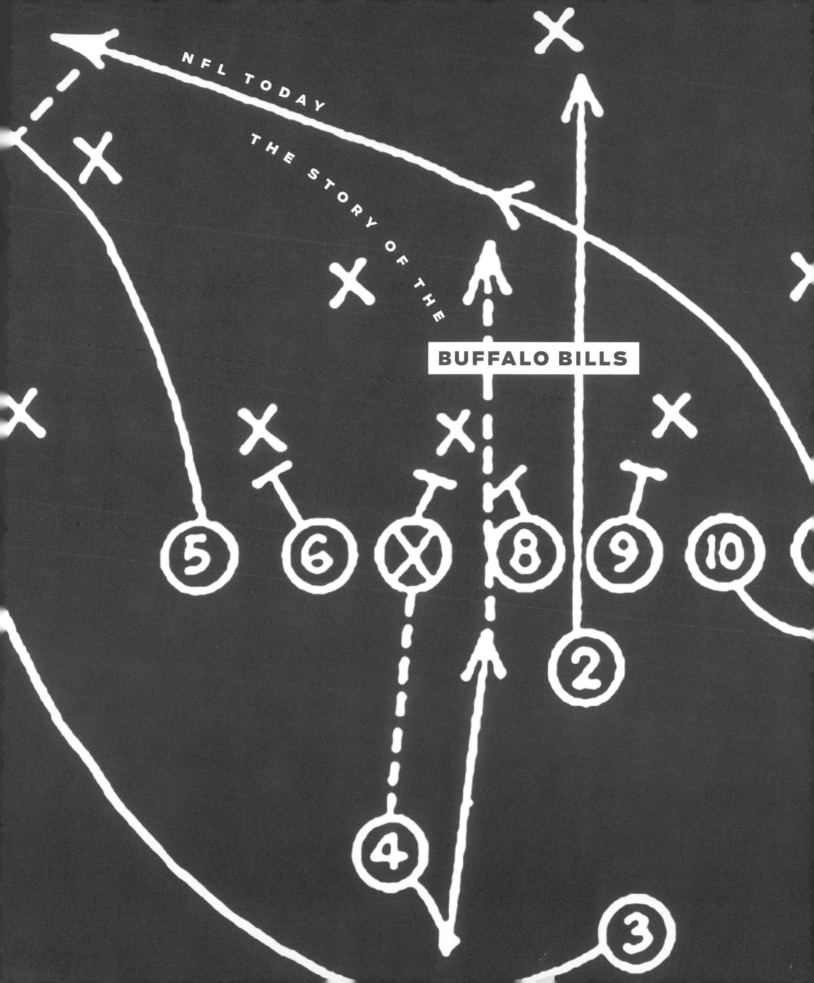

NFL TODAY

THE STORY OF THE

BUFFALO BILLS

NFL TODAY

THE STORY OF THE BUFFALO BILLS

SARA GILBERT

CREATIVE EDUCATION

PUBLISHED BY CREATIVE EDUCATION
P.O. BOX 227, MANKATO, MINNESOTA 56002
CREATIVE EDUCATION IS AN IMPRINT OF THE CREATIVE COMPANY
WWW.THECREATIVECOMPANY.US

DESIGN AND PRODUCTION BY BLUE DESIGN
ART DIRECTION BY RITA MARSHALL
PRINTED IN THE UNITED STATES OF AMERICA

PHOTOGRAPHS BY ALAMY (CULLIGANPHOTO, LARRY
B. REED), GETTY IMAGES (SYLVIA ALLEN/NFL, DOUG
BENC, SCOTT BOEHM, DAVID DERMER/DIAMOND
IMAGES, DIAMOND IMAGES, ELSA, FOCUS ON SPORT,
ANDY HAYT, GEORGE LONG/SPORTS ILLUSTRATED, G.
NEWMAN LOWRANCE, AL MESSERSCHMIDT, RONALD C.
MODRA/SPORTS IMAGERY, NFL, HY PESKIN/SPORTS
ILLUSTRATED, GEORGE ROSE, JOHN RUTHROFF/AFP,
HERB SCHARFMAN/SPORTS IMAGERY, RICH SCHULTZ,
PAUL SPINELLI, RICK STEWART, RICK STEWART/
ALLSPORT, MATT SULLIVAN, TOM SZCZERBOWSKI,
CHARLES AQUA VIVA, HERBERT WEITMAN/NFL
PHOTOS, LOU WITT/NFL)

LIBRARY OF CONGRESS CATALOGING-IN-PUBLICATION DATA
THE STORY OF THE BUFFALO BILLS / SARA GILBERT.
P. CM. — (NFL TODAY)
INCLUDES INDEX.
SUMMARY: THE HISTORY OF THE NATIONAL FOOTBALL LEAGUE'S
BUFFALO BILLS, SURVEYING THE FRANCHISE'S BIGGEST STARS
AND MOST MEMORABLE MOMENTS FROM ITS INAUGURAL SEASON
IN 1960 TO TODAY.
ISBN 978-1-60818-295-4
1. BUFFALO BILLS (FOOTBALL TEAM)—HISTORY—JUVENILE
LITERATURE.

GV956.B83S86 2013
796.332'640974797—DC23      2012027216

FIRST EDITION
9 8 7 6 5 4 3 2 1

COVER: RUNNING BACK C. J. SPILLER
PAGE 2: WIDE RECEIVER STEVIE JOHNSON
PAGES 4—5: 2007 BUFFALO BILLS
PAGE 6: DEFENSIVE LINEMEN MARIO WILLIAMS AND MARCELL
DAREUS

# TABLE OF CONTENTS

BUFFALO IS CALLED THE "CITY OF GOOD NEIGHBORS" AND "CITY OF LIGHT"

# Bills in Buffalo

**B**uffalo is the second-largest city in the state of New York, ranking behind only New York City in population figures. Its location on the shores of Lake Erie, just 17 miles south of the spectacular Niagara Falls, makes it a beautiful and busy port city. It is home to several large colleges and universities that educate students from all over the country; it also draws many visitors from nearby Canada. The city of more than a million people is so hospitable that national publications have in recent years ranked it as America's 2nd-best city to relocate to, the 6th-most energetic city, and the 10th-best place to raise a family in the United States.

Buffalo has also proven to be one of the best places in the country to build a professional football franchise. The city's football tradition began in 1946, when the Buffalo Bisons started playing as part of the All-America Football Conference (AAFC). The Bisons posted a disappointing 3–10–1 record in their first—and only—season. By the time the 1947 season started, the Bisons had been renamed the Buffalo Bills, after

THE FIRST BILLS TEAMS PLAYED HOME GAMES AT WAR MEMORIAL STADIUM

# Ralph Wilson

**TEAM OWNER / BILLS SEASONS: 1959—PRESENT**

Through 2012, Ralph Wilson was the only owner the non-AAFC Buffalo Bills had ever had. Wilson understood early on that in order for the Bills to survive, the American Football League (AFL) had to thrive. So he helped devise the AFL's revenue-sharing plan, which assisted other teams' profitability in the 1960s. Collecting funds from ticket sales and television rights, teams had a pool of money to use in different ways—from player signings to stadium repairs. "I don't think a lot of people realize the amount of money Mr. Wilson pumped into the Bills in those early years in the AFL," Bills defensive lineman Tom Day later said. "I don't think Mr. Wilson ever intended to move the Bills to any place other than Buffalo." By 2012, Wilson continued to spearhead the NFL's revenue-sharing plan, and his commitment to his team was matched only by his feelings for the Buffalo community at large. "He cares about the area as well as the football team," former general manager Marv Levy said. "And there is nothing that would make him happier than to see the Bills win a Super Bowl."

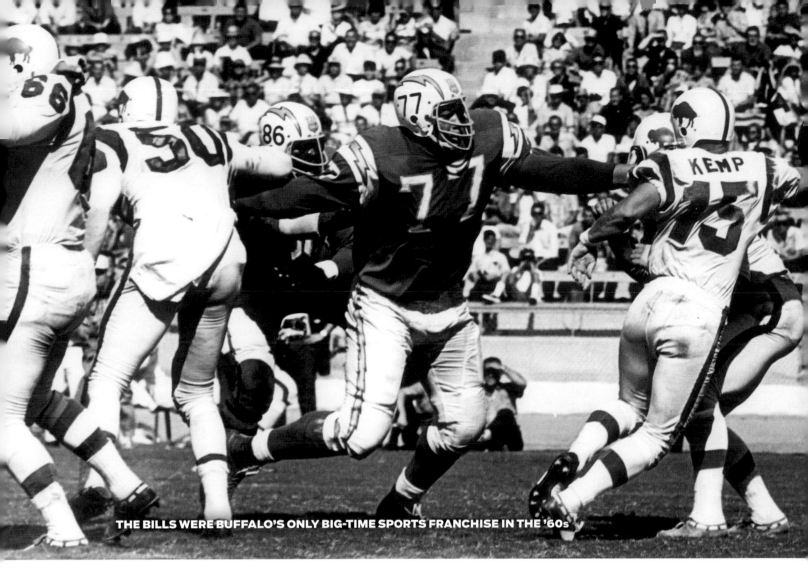

THE BILLS WERE BUFFALO'S ONLY BIG-TIME SPORTS FRANCHISE IN THE '60s

notorious Wild West hunter, showman, and sharpshooter William "Buffalo Bill" Cody.

The reloaded Bills, featuring rookie quarterback George Ratterman, came out shooting in 1947 and blazed their way to an 8–4–2 record. The next year, with halfback Chet Mutryn scoring 15 touchdowns, Buffalo locked up first place in the league's Eastern Division. The Bills topped the Baltimore Colts 28–17 in the Division Championship Game but fell to the undefeated Cleveland Browns, 49–7, in a lopsided AAFC Championship Game.

But 1949 was a bad year for both the Bills, who dropped to fourth place in their division, and the AAFC, which ended operations at the close of the season. Most of the AAFC teams folded, although three of them—the Browns, Colts, and San Francisco 49ers—joined the National Football League (NFL) in 1950. Buffalo had enjoyed more success on the field and in ticket sales than many of the NFL teams, but team owner Jim Breuli decided that the team would fold rather than join the NFL.

Buffalo's football fans waited patiently for most of a decade to have a team of their own to cheer for. Finally, in 1960, a wealthy Texas businessman named Lamar Hunt gathered seven other millionaires and

# "It feels great to give them a championship."

WRAY CARLTON

established the American Football League (AFL) after being denied franchise ownership opportunities in the NFL. One of those millionaires was Ralph Wilson, a minority owner of the NFL's Detroit Lions. Trusted Lions colleagues convinced Wilson that Buffalo should be his top choice as a location for a new franchise because its fans were still hungry for football. After holding a public team-naming contest, Wilson resurrected the Bills name, and Buffalo had football back in the form of a new AFL franchise.

During those first days, Wilson did just about everything himself, including drafting players. "We had a hat, and we put the names on little pieces of paper and dropped them in…," he said about the AFL's draft process. "If you wanted a quarterback, you reached in the quarterback hat and drew out a name." That's how he found "Riverboat Richie" Lucas, the first player ever drafted by the Bills.

Wilson's selection of the team's first coach was more strategic. He reached back to his Detroit days to hire defensive coordinator Buster Ramsey in 1960. Despite Ramsey's brilliant defensive innovations, including the use of blitzing linebackers, and running back Wray Carlton's nose for the end zone, the Bills suffered through two straight losing seasons. Ramsey was fired, and player personnel director Lou Saban was promoted to head coach.

Saban took chances on undrafted players such as cornerback Booker Edgerson, journeyman quarterback Jack Kemp, and Canadian Football League running back Carlton "Cookie" Gilchrist. In 1962, Gilchrist became the AFL's first 1,000-yard rusher. His 13 rushing touchdowns also set the all-time AFL record, making Gilchrist an easy choice as the AFL's Most Valuable Player (MVP). The following year, led by Gilchrist's bruising running, Saban's fiery leadership, and kicker and defensive end Mack Yoho's two-way play, Buffalo made the playoffs. Although they got thumped by the Boston Patriots 26–8, the Bills were starting to roll.

With one of the best defenses in the league and an explosive offense, Buffalo started 1964 with nine straight wins and finished with a 12–2 record. The Bills advanced to their first AFL Championship Game, where defensive tackle Tom Sestak and a ferocious line dismantled the San Diego Chargers' passing game. Kemp sealed the 20–7 Bills win with a game-ending quarterback sneak. Afterward, the players felt

# These Bills Look Like Lions

Ralph Wilson was a minority owner of the Detroit Lions for a decade before taking ownership of the Bills in 1959. He looked to Detroit for his first head coach—defensive coordinator Buster Ramsey—and asked the coach to design the team's uniforms. All Ramsey knew was the Lions, so his design basically had the Bills wearing Lions uniforms. "The Bills were a duplicate of the Detroit Lions," trainer Eddie Abramoski said, "starting with the Honolulu blue and silver uniforms." Buffalo uniforms featured blue jerseys with silver trim and pants at home, and white jerseys with blue trim on the road. The helmets also mimicked Detroit's, with a silver base and blue numerals on the sides. When former Boston Patriots coach Lou Saban took over as Buffalo's coach in 1962, he also designed new uniforms that resembled those of his former team. As Bills reporter Jack Horrigan of the *Buffalo Evening News* explained, "Saban decided to 'brighten up' the Bills' new uniforms by adding scarlet and making more use of white than the former silver-blue combination."

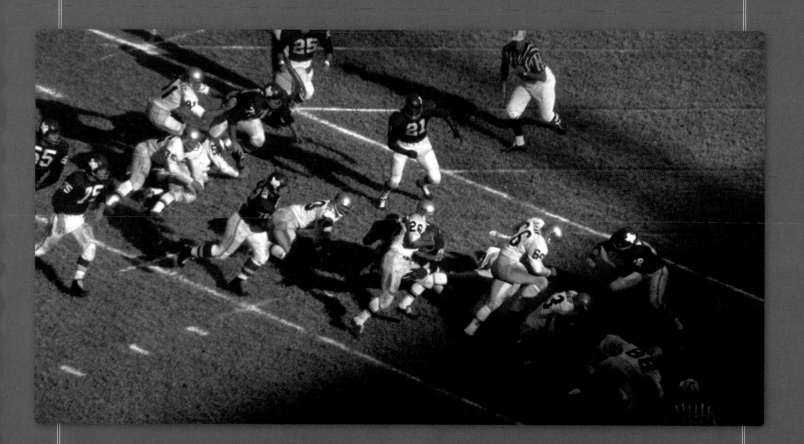

**EARLY BLUE-AND-SILVER BILLS IN ACTION AGAINST THE DALLAS TEXANS**

proud to win for their faithful fans. "The city accepted us and supported us when we were down," said Carlton. "It feels great to give them a championship."

n 1965, the Bills were the team to beat in the AFL. There were few individual standouts as Coach Saban led a balanced, tight-knit team that only got stronger as it charged toward an AFL Championship Game rematch with San Diego. This one was no contest. Kemp threw an early touchdown pass to Ernie Warlick, and Butch Byrd ran a 74-yard punt into the end zone before halftime. In the second half, kicker Pete Gogolak booted three field goals. The defense smothered the Chargers' offense in a convincing 23–0 shutout. Then, just a week after the championship repeat, Saban shocked everyone by resigning as coach.

THE BILLS CRUSHED THE CHARGERS IN BOTH OF THEIR AFL TITLE GAME CLASHES

# Jack Kemp

QUARTERBACK / BILLS SEASONS: 1962–69 / HEIGHT: 6-FOOT-1 / WEIGHT: 201 POUNDS

Jack Kemp was involved in one of pro football's first quarterback controversies. After the Buffalo offense stalled in 1964, Kemp was benched in the second-to-last game of the season against the Denver Broncos. With Buffalo facing a must-win situation against the Boston Patriots the next week to decide the Eastern Division's representative in the AFL Championship Game, Kemp sat next to coach Lou Saban on the plane ride home and spoke up. "I told Saban if he wanted to win he had to play me.... I wasn't putting down [backup quarterback Daryle] Lamonica at all, because he made me a better quarterback, but I told Saban, 'If you start me, I guarantee I'll win this game for you.'" Kemp did start and scored on two quarterback sneaks as Buffalo trumped Boston 24–14. Such leadership and follow-through eventually enabled Kemp to cofound the AFL's Players' Association and become its five-time president. It also compelled him to successfully seek a seat in the United States House of Representatives (serving from 1971 to 1989) and to run as Republican presidential nominee Bob Dole's vice presidential mate in 1996.

# Western Name for an Eastern Team

The city of Buffalo, New York, was never part of the Wild West. It was never part of Buffalo Bill Cody's history, either. But when the owner of a new football team in the city in 1946 solicited ideas for a new name from the people of Buffalo, the winning suggestion was to name the team after the famous western soldier, hunter, and showman. The name was so popular that when another new team came to town in 1960, it was again named the Bills. But instead of connecting to their actual namesake—Buffalo Bill—the Buffalo Bills have built their image around the American bison, which is often referred to as a buffalo. The logo on their helmet is a buffalo, and the team mascot is a buffalo. The closest connection to Buffalo Bill himself is the name of the team's cheerleading squad: the Buffalo Jills. Of course, Buffalo Bill is well known for his own connection to buffalo. He was an accomplished hunter who claimed to have killed more than 4,000 of the once-abundant animal within a 17-month period.

THE BILLS CELEBRATED THE AFL'S 50TH ANNIVERSARY WITH THROWBACK UNIFORMS IN 2009

# Running with the Juice

**S**aban's replacement, Joe Collier, inherited a multitalented team that marched easily to a third straight title game. This time, however, Buffalo faced the powerful Kansas City Chiefs, who handed the Bills a crushing 31–7 loss on New Year's Day. Things started to unravel in Buffalo after that. The Bills finished the 1967 season at 4–10. Then, during the 1968 preseason, Kemp suffered a season-ending knee injury. When the Bills started 0–2 again, Collier was fired. Buffalo limped to a 1–12–1 record in what became known as "The Dark Season."

The bright side to Buffalo's decline was that the team got the number-one overall pick in the 1969 AFL Draft, which it used on University of Southern California running back Orenthal James (O. J.) Simpson, who had won the Heisman Trophy as college football's best player. Nicknamed "The Juice," Simpson was barely

O. J. SIMPSON BECAME A FOUR-TIME NFL RUSHING CHAMPION IN THE '70s

# ✕Joe DeLamielleure

**GUARD / BILLS SEASONS: 1973–79, 1985 / HEIGHT: 6-FOOT-3 / WEIGHT: 254 POUNDS**

After being selected in the first round of the 1973 NFL Draft by the Bills, Joe DeLamielleure immediately commanded respect. "Mr. Wilson still tells me that to this day I am the only player he personally called to inform that I had been drafted by Buffalo," DeLamielleure later wrote in his autobiography. An immediate starter his rookie season, "Joe D" went on to win All-Rookie honors and to become one of the team's greatest offensive linemen ever. Known for his brilliant run blocking, the swift-pulling DeLamielleure was also a deft pass blocker. Durable and dependable, he played in 185 consecutive games in 13 seasons with the Bills and the Cleveland Browns. "As I matured as a player, I realized that it took more brains than brawn to keep playing," he said. "I probably went downhill physically during my later years, but I played better because I got smarter. [Oakland Raiders linebacker] Ted Hendricks told me to 'stay low, keep your feet moving, and avoid any pileups.' And over time I added one more tip—play until the whistle blows." DeLamielleure left Buffalo in 1979 but returned for his final season in 1985.

# "There's your meal ticket. Go block for him."

LOU SABAN ON O. J. SIMPSON

used by new coach John Rauch, who preferred to move the ball by air rather than by ground. That unbalanced offense contributed to a meager 4–10 record. Then, when the AFL and NFL merged in 1970, things got worse for Buffalo, as it dropped to a 3–10–1 record. Buffalo hit rock bottom in 1971, winning just one game all season.

After that season, a frustrated Simpson considered quitting the game. But then Lou Saban returned as head coach. His plan to revive the team involved running the ball—a lot. After handing the ball to Simpson during practice, Coach Saban said to his offensive linemen, "There's your meal ticket. Go block for him." And block they did. Buffalo's offensive line—center Bruce Jarvis, guards Reggie McKenzie and Joe DeLamielleure, and tackles Donnie Green and Dave Foley—grew so skilled at opening holes that they became known as the "Electric Company" because they "turned on The Juice." Simpson ran for 1,251 yards in 1972.

Simpson's dominance inspired confidence among his teammates, who started the 1973 season eager to see how many yards he could cover. McKenzie boldly predicted that Simpson would rush for 2,000 yards—breaking the record of 1,863 yards held by Simpson's idol, Cleveland Browns fullback Jim Brown.

When The Juice cracked a rib in practice and wasn't able to play in any preseason games, that prophecy appeared to be in doubt. The time spent resting paid off, though. Simpson opened the season by gaining a then NFL-record 250 yards in a 31–13 win over the New England Patriots. He gained more than 100 yards in each of his next 4 games as well. On December 16, during a snowy afternoon game against the New York Jets, Simpson lived up to McKenzie's expectations by rushing for

# Football Meets Soccer

Pete Gogolak is responsible for a lot of football "firsts." He was the first placekicker ever drafted by the Bills (in 1964), the first "soccer-style" kicker in professional football, and the first player to jump from the AFL to the NFL. "Nobody had ever seen anybody kick the ball this way," Gogolak later recalled. "Before that, [Buffalo] never, ever carried a kicking specialist. Basically, Buffalo took a chance on me." Buffalo took a chance, but quarterback Jack Kemp wasn't about to risk getting his throwing hand kicked, leaving holding duties to backup quarterback Daryle Lamonica. "No one had ever held for a soccer-style kicker, but he knew exactly how he wanted the ball," Lamonica said. "His ball just exploded and got great height. Nobody could jump up and block it. He was a real asset." Gogolak helped the Bills win back-to-back AFL championships over the San Diego Chargers in 1964 and 1965. The second championship was Gogolak's finale with the Bills. Four months later, he became the first AFL player to cross over to the NFL, joining the New York Giants.

**PETE GOGOLAK EARNED A TRIP TO THE AFL PRO BOWL AFTER THE 1965 SEASON**

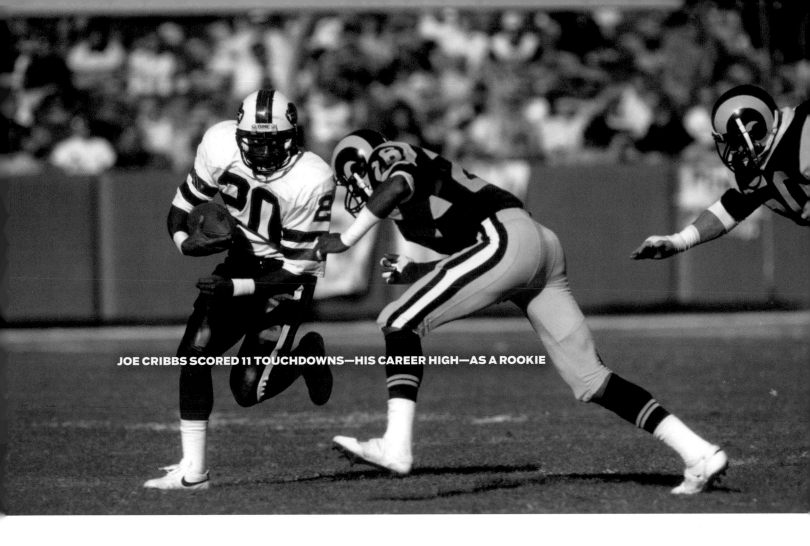

JOE CRIBBS SCORED 11 TOUCHDOWNS—HIS CAREER HIGH—AS A ROOKIE

200 yards, pushing his total for the season to 2,003 yards—and becoming the first NFL running back to achieve such a feat.

Although Simpson continued to overpower opposing defenses, Buffalo wasn't the powerhouse Saban had hoped it would be. After missing the 1975 playoffs and then falling to a 2–12 record in 1976, Saban left again. Team owner Ralph Wilson hired Chuck Knox, who had led the Los Angeles Rams to five consecutive division titles, to take over. Knox had earned the nickname "Ground Chuck" because he had always relied on a strong running game to win, but he recognized right away that Simpson was too old and injury prone to be effective much longer. He traded The Juice to the 49ers for five draft picks over three years, which he used to select players such as wide receiver Jerry Butler and scrappy linebacker Jim Haslett. By 1980, Knox had laid the foundation for a new era of hope in Buffalo.

Knox built his rushing attack around Joe Cribbs, a 5-foot-11 and 190-pound running back who some believed was too small to be effective. But Cribbs proved them wrong by rushing for more than 1,000

SMALL BUT FAST, JERRY BUTLER SPECIALIZED IN HAULING IN LONG PASSES

yards in 3 of his first 4 seasons. "What they didn't measure on Joe was his toughness," said nose tackle Fred Smerlas. "Pound for pound, Joe was the toughest guy in the league." Thanks largely to Cribbs and a rugged defense that featured linebackers Isiah Robertson and Phil Villapiano, the Bills made the playoffs two years in a row. But they were knocked out by the Chargers in 1980 and the Cincinnati Bengals in 1981.

The momentum Buffalo had built was lost in 1982, when a players' strike shortened the season. Soon after, both Knox and Cribbs left the team. The losses mounted during three subsequent losing seasons. "We were so bad," Smerlas later joked, "the only thing that showed up at Rich Stadium on Sundays were the snowflakes."

Midway through a horrid 1986 season, Wilson hired new coach Marv Levy, whose optimistic and enthusiastic attitude was a breath of fresh air for the downtrodden Bills. His first key decision was to sign Houston Oilers reserve receiver Steve Tasker, a diminutive player who epitomized Levy's hardworking, team-first philosophy by becoming a special teams star. "When we were down, Marv showed us the way up," Tasker said.

## The Buffalo Curse

"The Buffalo Curse" is a mythical explanation for Buffalo's professional sports teams' inability to win league championships. After winning two AFL championships in the mid-1960s, the Bills have never won the Super Bowl. Likewise, the Sabres of the National Hockey League have never won a Stanley Cup, despite several close calls. The alleged curse really seemed to take hold in 1990 after kicker Scott Norwood's failed last-second field goal attempt handed the Giants a Super Bowl XXV victory. The Bills lost three more Super Bowls after that (following the 1991, 1992, and 1993 seasons). Then, from 1994 through 2012, the Bills won only one playoff game. There are a couple of notable curse theories. One legend explains that Seneca Indian chief Red Jacket once put a curse on the entire city. Another notes the assassination of former president William McKinley at Buffalo's Pan-American Exposition in 1901. A January 2008 chant ceremony led by a paranormalist named Mason C. Winfield III claimed to have lifted the curse for good. "Put off your aches, your pains, your ills," the chant went. "God bless our Sabres and our Bills."

**FEW TEAMS HAVE SUFFERED AS MANY PAINFUL NEAR MISSES AS THE BILLS**

**BRUCE SMITH WAS A LONGTIME NIGHTMARE FOR OPPOSING QUARTERBACKS**

# Stymied in the Super Bowl

**L**evy showed the 1988 Bills the way up the division standings by getting them their first American Football Conference (AFC) East Division title in eight seasons. Four key players led the way: defensive end Bruce Smith, receiver Andre Reed, quarterback Jim Kelly, and Thurman Thomas, a running back who arrived in Buffalo in 1988. A multitalented athlete, Thomas was a superb runner and receiver who did all the little things that helped the Bills win. His blocking skills set him apart from the competition, and he was widely considered to be one of the best backs at stopping blitzing defenders.

With all that talent on the roster, the Bills were ready to run wild. Kelly led what was known as the "K-Gun" offense, in which he lined up in the shotgun formation (several yards behind the center) to either hand off to Thomas or fire passes to Reed. The offense also often ran plays without breaking to huddle, which exhausted opposing

JIM KELLY COOLLY LED A FAST-PACED OFFENSE DURING THE BILLS' GLORY YEARS

# Jim Kelly

**QUARTERBACK / BILLS SEASONS: 1986–96 / HEIGHT: 6-FOOT-3 / WEIGHT: 225 POUNDS**

It was sometimes said that Jim Kelly was "a quarterback with a linebacker's mentality." There are many examples of his toughness. But one home game in 1990 against the Phoenix Cardinals captured it best. After being hit in the jaw by blitzing Phoenix safety Leonard Smith, Kelly went down and fumbled the ball. A Cardinals defensive lineman scooped it up and ran with it. After the lineman finally was brought down, the referees separated players from the pile. There, at the bottom of the pile, was Kelly, still tussling with the bigger lineman for the ball. He lost the ball but gained even more respect from his teammates. "Like Babe Ruth was to the [New York] Yankees and Michael Jordan was to the [Chicago] Bulls, Jim Kelly is to the Bills," Bills receiver Steve Tasker once wrote. "He taught us how to win and, in the process, saved the franchise." Kelly was so respected that coach Marv Levy and offensive coordinator Ted Marchibroda treated the Hall-of-Famer like an on-field coach. They valued his opinion about personnel, play calls, and team decisions as much as that of any team executive.

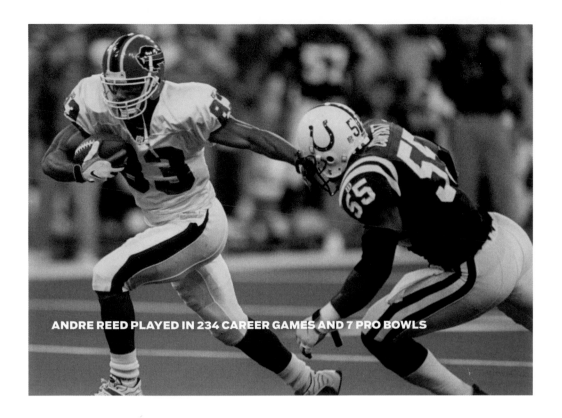
ANDRE REED PLAYED IN 234 CAREER GAMES AND 7 PRO BOWLS

defenses. On defense, meanwhile, Smith was tireless in his pursuit of opposing quarterbacks, posting 10 or more sacks per season in 12 of his 15 years in Buffalo. With linebackers Darryl Talley and Cornelius Bennett also wreaking havoc, the Bills were ready to rule the AFC.

In 1990, the Bills nearly doubled the combined scoring output of their opponents (428–263) and then romped over two teams in the playoffs, including a 51–3 destruction of the Los Angeles Raiders in the AFC Championship Game. But in Super Bowl XXV against the New York Giants, Buffalo's momentum was thwarted by a New York team that had possession of the ball more than twice as long as Buffalo did. With the Giants leading 20–19 and just 4 seconds left on the clock, Bills kicker Scott Norwood lined up for a 47-yard field goal that would have captured the Bills' first NFL championship. Instead, it sailed wide right. "That ball slid by that upright by about a foot," Kelly said sadly. "We were a foot away from being champions."

In 1991, Buffalo's offense was even better. Kelly passed for 3,844 yards and 33 touchdowns as the Bills marched to another shot at Super Bowl glory. But Thomas, who had accounted for more than 2,000 total yards in the regular season, inexplicably disappeared in Super Bowl XXVI against the Washington Redskins. After misplacing his helmet and missing the game's opening series, Thomas fizzled. The star running back posted just 13 rushing yards, and Buffalo again came up short, this time 37–24.

Buffalo remained the AFC's top squad in 1992. After backup quarterback Frank Reich directed a monumental 41–38 comeback win over the Houston Oilers in the first round of the playoffs, Buffalo

THURMAN THOMAS WAS VERY DURABLE FOR A RUSHER, PLAYING 13 SEASONS

cruised through the next two rounds. But the Bills were once again outmatched in the Super Bowl, this time losing 52–17 to the Dallas Cowboys.

In 1993, Buffalo set an NFL record by advancing to its fourth consecutive Super Bowl—a highly anticipated rematch with Dallas. After kicker Steve Christie boomed a Super Bowl–record 54-yard field goal in the first quarter, the Bills marched to a 13–6 halftime lead. But they never scored another point, and Dallas pulled away to win 30–13. Despite the agony of experiencing four straight Super Bowl losses, Wilson remained proud. "No matter what the scoreboard said," he said, "this team was a champion in my heart."

After 1994, even excellent efforts from such players as linebacker Bryce Paup couldn't get the Bills back to the Super Bowl. Kelly retired in 1996 after a demoralizing 30–27 playoff loss to the

# The Backup's Comeback

In 1984, quarterback Frank Reich was responsible for what was then the biggest comeback in the history of college football. As the backup to Stan Gelbaugh at the University of Maryland, Reich stepped in and led the Terrapins out of a first-half 31–0 hole to a 42–40 victory over the previously unbeaten University of Miami. So when the Bills called on Reich in a 1992 playoff game against the Houston Oilers to replace an injured Jim Kelly, he already had some come-from-behind mojo working in his favor. Consistently connecting with wide receiver Andre Reed, Reich led the Bills back from a 35–3 deficit to a sensational 41–38 victory. Kicker Steve Christie booted the winning field goal in overtime to cap what was still the largest comeback in NFL history as of 2012. Reich also started the next week in a playoff matchup in Pittsburgh against the Steelers, leading Buffalo to a 24–3 win. "The guys on this team were so encouraging," Reich said. "They kept me up when it could have been real easy to get down."

**FRANK REICH STARTED ONLY EIGHT GAMES IN NINE YEARS AS A BILLS BACKUP**

STEADY KICKER STEVE CHRISTIE BOOTED 234 FIELD GOALS FOR BUFFALO

Jacksonville Jaguars. Levy departed after a 6–10 season in 1997, and eventually Thomas, Smith, and Reed each moved on as well. "We were blessed to have a core of guys who gave it everything they had, every Sunday," Levy said. "It was an honor to lead such men."

Levy's replacement, Wade Phillips, built a winning team that went 10–6 in 1998 and 11–5 in 1999. Quarterback Doug Flutie and sure-handed receiver Eric Moulds led the Bills to the playoffs as a Wild Card contender both years. The 1999 playoff game against the Tennessee Titans was a heartbreaker. With just 16 seconds remaining on the clock and a 16–15 lead on the scoreboard, Buffalo kicked off to Tennessee. A Titans blocker handed the ball to tight end Frank Wycheck, who fired a long, cross-field lateral to receiver Kevin Dyson. Dyson then sprinted 75 yards for an amazing touchdown that won the game. "My heart sank when I saw that guy cross the goal line," said Bills defensive end Phil Hansen. "I thought the game was in the bag."

After Buffalo fell to 8–8 in 2000, Phillips was fired. New coach Gregg Williams oversaw a 3–13 season in 2001. Seeking a boost, Buffalo traded with the Patriots for star quarterback Drew Bledsoe. With Bledsoe orchestrating the offense and running back Travis Henry galloping for 1,438 yards, the Bills climbed back to 8–8 in 2002. Despite opening the 2003 season with a 31–0 win over the Patriots and having a talented defense led by hard-hitting linebacker Takeo Spikes, Buffalo dropped to 6–10. The season ended with a 31–0 loss to the same Patriots the Bills had routed to start the season.

RECEIVER ERIC MOULDS WAS A PRO-BOWLER IN 1998, 2000, AND 2002

THE 2004 BILLS DEFENSE ROSE UP AS ONE OF THE LEAGUE'S FIERCEST

# Bringing in New Bills

**A**ttempting to stop the downward slide, the Bills brought in a new coach—Mike Mularkey—and a new quarterback—J. P. Losman—in 2004. Although Losman was supposed to relieve the struggling Bledsoe under center, he broke his leg in the preseason and missed most of the regular season. The lackluster Bills started the season 0–4 but seemed to find their groove after a 20–13 win over the Miami Dolphins in Week 5. Rookie running back Willis McGahee made an immediate impression by charging for more than 1,000 yards, scoring 13 touchdowns, and helping the Bills win 8 of their last 11 games.

With his best years as a quarterback behind him, Bledsoe left Buffalo before the 2005 season. But Losman, who had been pegged as his replacement, faltered in his first four games as a starter. Backup quarterback Kelly Holcomb stepped in, but neither he nor McGahee could salvage the season for the Bills. When the team finished with a miserable 5–11 record, the general manager was fired and, after only two years at the

STAR TAKEO SPIKES SCORED TWO DEFENSIVE TOUCHDOWNS IN 2004

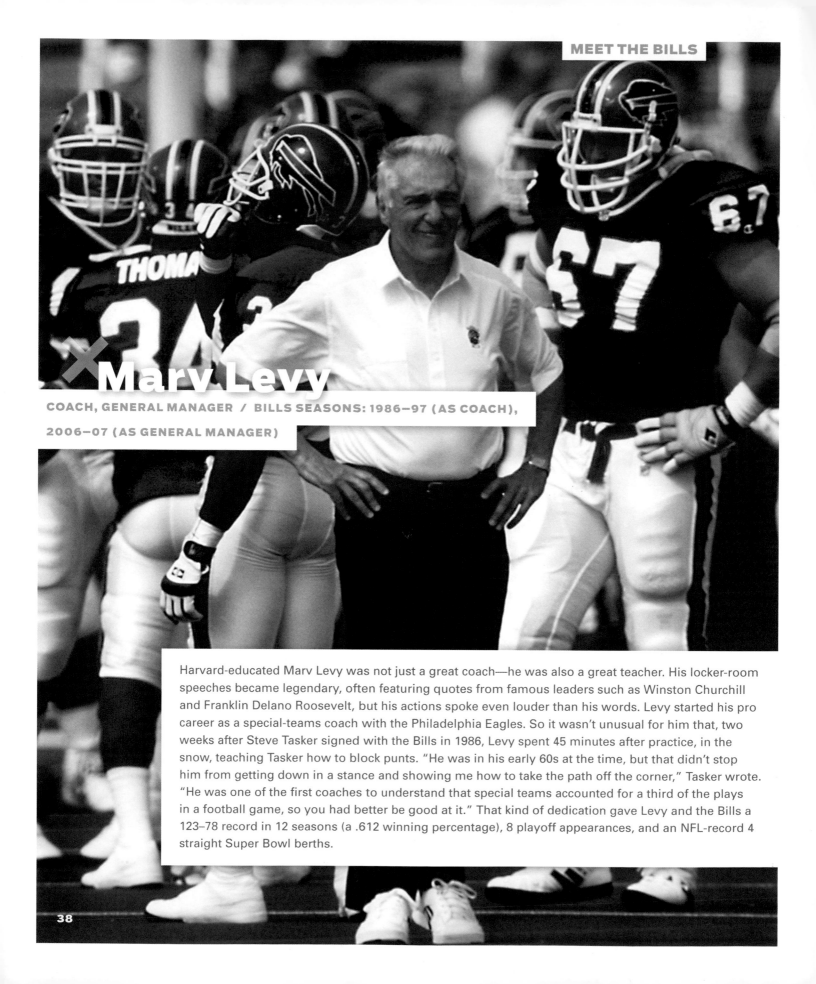

# Marv Levy

COACH, GENERAL MANAGER / BILLS SEASONS: 1986–97 (AS COACH), 2006–07 (AS GENERAL MANAGER)

Harvard-educated Marv Levy was not just a great coach—he was also a great teacher. His locker-room speeches became legendary, often featuring quotes from famous leaders such as Winston Churchill and Franklin Delano Roosevelt, but his actions spoke even louder than his words. Levy started his pro career as a special-teams coach with the Philadelphia Eagles. So it wasn't unusual for him that, two weeks after Steve Tasker signed with the Bills in 1986, Levy spent 45 minutes after practice, in the snow, teaching Tasker how to block punts. "He was in his early 60s at the time, but that didn't stop him from getting down in a stance and showing me how to take the path off the corner," Tasker wrote. "He was one of the first coaches to understand that special teams accounted for a third of the plays in a football game, so you had better be good at it." That kind of dedication gave Levy and the Bills a 123–78 record in 12 seasons (a .612 winning percentage), 8 playoff appearances, and an NFL-record 4 straight Super Bowl berths.

helm, Mularkey announced his resignation in January 2006.

**D**ick Jauron was hired to replace Mularkey, but it was the man who had been recruited to fill the vacant general manager spot who attracted the most attention in Buffalo: Marv Levy, the winningest coach in team history. Fans hoped that Levy would be able to work the same magic as general manager that he had as a coach during Buffalo's string of successes in the 1990s. But after the Bills finished both the 2006 and 2007 campaigns with identical 7–9 records, well out of the playoff picture, the 82-year-old Levy retired. "I was sad to hear the news that he was leaving," said young quarterback Trent Edwards, whom Levy had selected in the third round of the 2007 Draft. "But I think

MARSHAWN LYNCH COMBINED SPEED, TOUGHNESS, AND FLASH

he's left this organization much better off than before he came here."

Despite Levy's departure, Buffalo fans had a reason to be optimistic at the start of the 2008 season. Edwards had shown promise taking over for Losman in 2007 and helped the Bills jump out to a surprising 4–0 start in 2008. The offense, led by swift receiver Lee Evans and flashy halfback Marshawn Lynch, showed some potential for explosiveness, while young linebacker Paul Posluszny and defensive end Aaron Schobel looked to resurrect Buffalo's tradition of a stout defense. But then Edwards took a huge hit in a game against the Arizona Cardinals and suffered a concussion. Although he was able to return for the next game, both he and the Bills had far less wind in their sails. The season again ended with a disappointing 7–9 record.

The Bills made headlines before the 2009 season started by signing veteran wide receiver Terrell Owens to a one-year contract. Owens's talent as a receiver was rivaled only by his creativity in the end zone when celebrating touchdowns, and the Bills hoped his energy could lift them back into contention. But his arrival in Buffalo seemed to have the opposite effect. Owens's performance was subpar, and the Bills stumbled through an ugly 6–10 season that saw Jauron get fired and Edwards battle injuries.

The flurry of personnel changes that ensued left the Bills with Chan Gailey as their new coach but without Owens or Edwards for most of the 2010 season. Ryan Fitzpatrick performed admirably at

# Stampeding into Toronto

In his 2007 state of the league address, NFL commissioner Roger Goodell confirmed that the Buffalo Bills would play five regular-season games and three preseason games in Toronto, Ontario, over the following five years. The "Toronto Initiative" was to consist of one regular-season game being played at the Rogers Centre in downtown Toronto each year of the five-year pact, and one preseason game would be held there every other year. Goodell, a western New York native, was impressed by the Bills' proposal. "I think it was done very thoughtfully," he said. "I think it was done to help regionalize the team on an even broader scale than they have. They have regionalized throughout western New York, and that's helped the team be more successful from a business standpoint and market themselves more effectively. They have a tremendous amount of interest north into Canada and the Hamilton-Toronto area." Although the league had already played games in Mexico and London, England, by then, the Bills were set to blaze a trail—becoming the first NFL team to play at least one annual "home" game outside the U.S.

**ROGERS CENTRE HOSTS BOTH PROFESSIONAL BASEBALL AND FOOTBALL GAMES**

BILLS LINEMEN BLOCKED FOR A STRING OF DIFFERENT PASSERS IN THE 2000s

HALFBACK C. J. SPILLER ADDED BLISTERING SPEED TO THE BILLS' ATTACK

quarterback, and wide receiver Stevie Johnson scored 10 touchdowns for the team, but Buffalo lost its first eight games. When the Bills lost a heartbreaker to the Pittsburgh Steelers in overtime in Week 12, they were officially eliminated from playoff contention. Despite missing the postseason for the 11th straight year, Coach Gailey had hope for the future. "I think our players have a positive feeling about where we are and where we can be," he said when the season ended.

**B**uffalo's confidence was apparent when the 2011 season began with a 41–7 win over the Kansas City Chiefs. After starting out with an impressive 5–2 record, the Bills were decimated by injuries to several key players, including star nose tackle Kyle Williams, and the losses started piling up again. Fitzpatrick's development as a quarterback and the fancy footwork of running back Fred Jackson made it look like the Bills might finally make it back to the postseason for the first time since 1999. Unfortunately, the team's 6–10 record wasn't good enough for the playoffs, and Buffalo's playoff drought lingered.

# Bruce Smith

**DEFENSIVE END / BILLS SEASONS: 1985–99 / HEIGHT: 6-FOOT-4 / WEIGHT: 262 POUNDS**

After winning the Outland Trophy as America's top college lineman, Bruce Smith became the first overall pick of the 1985 NFL Draft. During his 15-year career with Buffalo, the "Sack Man" became one of the greatest NFL defensive players ever. An exceptionally quick and powerful pass rusher, Smith was also a superb run stuffer, often forcing opposing offenses to completely avoid his side of the field. In 1990, Smith tallied a career-high 19 sacks and won the first of 2 NFL Defensive Player of the Year awards (the other coming in 1996). Smith set a league record by notching at least 10 sacks in 13 seasons. When Buffalo cut him in 1999 to save money, Smith left with a heavy heart. "I wish I had the opportunity to play in front of our fans one more time, knowing that it was my last time," Smith said. "After 15 years in one place, the fans deserved better. I never got a chance to say goodbye." He ended his career with the Washington Redskins in 2003 as the NFL's all-time sacks leader (200).

A HARVARD GRADUATE, RYAN FITZPATRICK WAS KNOWN FOR HIS SMARTS

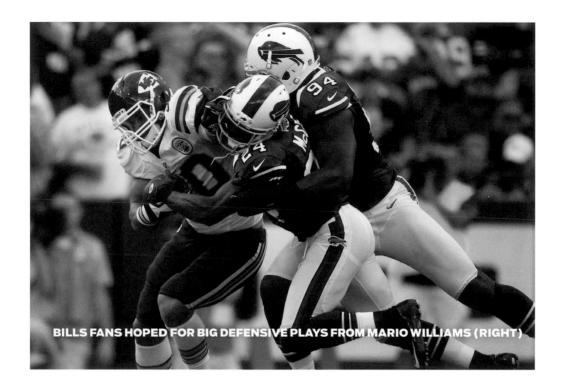

BILLS FANS HOPED FOR BIG DEFENSIVE PLAYS FROM MARIO WILLIAMS (RIGHT)

Despite the facts that the longest playoff drought in NFL history would turn out to continue in 2012 and that Jackson was frequently injured, running back C. J. Spiller filled in for his teammate and had the best season of his young career. Spiller rushed for 1,244 yards, scored 6 touchdowns, and was selected as an alternate to the Pro Bowl. Thankfully, Fitzpatrick did not replicate his league-leading number of interceptions (23) that he had made in 2011, but the Bills did post a win total (6) identical to the previous season's. In March 2013, Fitzpatrick left Buffalo for Tennessee, and the Bills looked to the NFL Draft for new possibilities.

During their long history, the Buffalo Bills have helped make northwestern New York a great place to live and visit. Although it's been a long time since their championship days in the AFL and their impressive run of 1990s Super Bowl appearances, Buffalo's hearty fans have remained loyal to their hometown team. No matter how long it takes, they still hold out hope that it won't be long before the Bills bring a Lombardi Trophy home to Buffalo.

# INDEX